EASY AIR FRYER COOKBOOK RECIPES

TASTY BEGINNER RECIPES FOR TWO WITH PICTURES

SHAHBAAZ AKHTAR

Copyright © 2018 by Shaz Publications

SHAZ Publications

Copyright@SHAZ Publications 2018

All Rights Reserved

No part of this publication may be reproduced,

transmitted or stored in a retrieval system, in any form or by any means,

without permission in writing from SHAZ Publications.

This book is sold subject to the condition that it shall not,

by way of trade or otherwise, be lent, resold, hired out or otherwise circulated

without the Publisher's prior consent in any form of binding or cover,

other than that in which it is published.

WHAT IS AN AIR FRYER AND HOW TO USE IT?

WHO CAN BENEFIT THE MOST FROM AN AIR FRYER?

HOW TO PREHEAT AIR FRYER?

A STEP-BY-STEP GUIDE AND A FEW THINGS TO KEEP IN MIND:

AIR FRYER FISH AND FRIES

AIR FRYER SPICY BARBECUE DRUMSTICKS

AIR FRYER ROASTED LAMB RACK

AIR FRYER HOT FRIED SHRIMPS

AIR FRYER CHICKEN BREAST

AIR FRYER CHICKEN STRIPS

AIR FRYER STUFFED CHEESE BURGER

AIR FRYER MEATBALLS

AIR FRYER AVOCADO FRIES

AIR FRYER MANCHURIAN CAULIFLOWER

AIR FRYER BOURBON BACON BURGERS

AIR FRYER SIMPLE FRENCH FRIES

AIR FRYER HOT DOGS

AIR FRYER HOT CHICKEN

AIR FRYER LEMON COOKIES

AIR FRYER THANKSGIVING TURKEY

AIR FRYER JALAPENO POPPERS

AIR FRYER CINNAMON ROLLS

AIR FRYER KOFTA KEBAB

AIR FRYER PEACH PIES

AIR FRYER PARCHMENT PAPER FISH

AIR FRYER ASPARAGUS FRIED

AIR FRYER BEETROOT CHIPS

AIR FRYER CAULIFLOWER NUGGETS

AIR FRYER TACO BELL WRAPS

AIR FRYER CALZONES

AIR FRYER PUMPKIN FRENCH FRIES

AIR FRYER WHOLE WHEAT PIZZA

AIR FRYER LAVA CAKES WITH PEPPERMINT

AIR FRYER WASABI CRAB CAKES

AIR FRYER SWEET POTATO FRIES

AIR FRYER ROASTED BROCCOLI WITH CHEESE SAUCE

AIR FRYER TURKEY BREAST

AIR FRYER BROWNIES

AIR FRYER MEXICAN STREET CORN

AIR FRYER KALE CRISP

AIR FRYER STUFFED PEPPERS

AIR FRYER DOUGHNUTS

AIR FRYER CHICKEN POPCORN

AIR FRYER FRIED RICE

AIR FRYER CRISPY ONION

AIR FRYER TOFU BROWN RICE

AIR FRYER POTATO CHIPS

AIR FRYER SHRIMP SPRING ROLLS

AIR FRYER BANANA CHIPS

AIR FRYER CHICKPEAS

AIR FRYER MONTE CRISTO

AIR FRYER NUTELLA SANDWICH

AIR FRYER SWEET POTATO WEDGES

AIR FRYER PIZZA BREAD STICKS

AIR FRYER APPLE CHIPS

AIR FRYER CHEESE STICKS

AIR FRYER ROASTED CARROTS

AIR FRYER CHOCOLATE CHIP COOKIE

AIR FRYER CHICKEN TENDER

AIR FRYER TOFU SALAD

AIR FRYER CHICKEN TIKKA

AIR FRYER SWEET POT TOT

AIR FRYER BANANA BREAD

AIR FRYER HASH BROWN

ABOUT AUTHOR

ONE LAST THING

Is it healthy to cook with an AIR FRYER?

Air Fryer are a healthy, guiltless way to enjoy your favourite fried food that have become increasingly popular lately.

They are designed to help reduce the fat content of popular foods like fries, chicken wings, empanadas and fish fingers.

What is an air fryer and how to use it?

A fryer is a popular kitchen appliance that cooks fried foods such as meat, pastries and potato chips.

It circulates hot air containing fine oil droplets around the food to create a crunchy and crispy appearance and taste.

This also results in a chemical reaction known as the Maillard effect which occurs in the presence of heat between an amino acid and a reducing sugar. This leads to changes in colour and taste of the food.

Air fried foods are a healthy alternative to fried foods thanks to their low-fat content and low caloric content.

Instead of dipping the food completely in the oil, you only need a tablespoon of oil for frying, to give the fried food a similar taste and a similar consistency.

Using an air fryer can help to reduce fat.

Deep-Fried foods are generally more fatty than foods made using other cooking methods.

For example, a chicken breast that has been fried contains about 30% more fat than the same amount of roasted chicken.

Some manufacturers claim that using a fryer can reduce the fat content of fried foods by 75%.

In fact, fryers require much less fat than traditional fryers. While many fried dishes require up to 3 cups (750 ml) of oil, air fryers only need 1 tablespoon (15 ml).

This means that deep fryers consume up to 50 times more oil than fryers and even if the oil is not completely absorbed by food, using an air fryer can significantly reduce fat content from your food.

A study compared the properties of deep-fried French fries and air fried French fries which showed that air frying resulted in a much lower fat end product with similar colour and moisture content.

This can have a significant impact on your health, as higher intake of vegetable oil fats has been linked to an increased risk of diseases such as heart disease and inflammation.

SUMMARY - Air fryers uses less oil than fryers and can produce foods with significantly lower fat content.

Moving to an air fryer can help you lose weight.

Air fried foods are not only lower in fat but also lower in calories and can contribute to weight loss.

A study of 33,542 Spanish adults showed that increased consumption of fried foods was associated with an increased risk of obesity.

If you want to cut your waistline, you can start by replacing your fried foods with air fried foods.

With 9 calories in every gram of fat, fats contain twice as many calories per gram as other macronutrients like proteins and carbohydrates.

Because air fried foods are less fatty than fried foods, switching to an air fryer can be an easy way to reduce calories and promote weight loss.

SUMMARY- Air fried Foods are less fatty than fried foods that can help reduce calorie intake and promote weight loss.

Compared to frying, using an air fryer can reduce the amount of fat, calories, and potentially harmful compounds in your food.

However, air-fried foods are still fried foods and their regular consumption can be associated with health problems.

Although fryers may be a better alternative to deep fryers, limiting your consumption of fried foods is the best option for your health.

Benefits of air frying?

I am sure you have seen the excitement (online) with fryers! These devices are undoubtedly the most popular and trendy thing of cooking this year. Maybe you are curious what the hype is about?

The first time I heard about it, I was also curious. Why are people so excited about these things? How can frying be healthy?

These devices are not fryers. They look more like a small independent convection oven. They use electrical elements to quickly heat the air, and then circulate that hot air around and through your food. This hot air cooks the food fast, making the food golden and crispy but the inside stays moist and delicious.

Advantages of cooking with an air fryer:

There are many reasons to use a fryer.

1. Cook healthier

So, how can frying be healthy? Easy! These units can be used without oil or with a small oil jet.

You can cook fries, onion rings, wings and more while getting really crisp results without extra oil. Compared to using my oven, the fries in the fryer were crisper but not dried out and their use to cook breaded zucchini was even more impressive!

2. Faster meals

Since they are smaller than an oven and circulate the air around with fans, they cook food faster. An oven may take 20 to 30 minutes to heat properly, these fryers reach the temperature in minutes.

I was very impressed with the fact that my frozen fries were perfect after 15 minutes while they were in the oven for up to 45 minutes. If you need to make snacks or meals in a hurry, you will save time.

3. Versatility

I think that's my favourite feature of an air fryer. You can do so much with it! Yes, it fries very well compared to an oven. But it can also bake (even cake), broil, roast, grill and stir fry! Do you want chicken and peas for dinner? Easy to cook them with one of these.

You can prepare fresh and frozen food and even reheat leftovers. I made meat, fish, pans, sandwiches and many different vegetables in mine. Some fryers have additional features, like a rotisserie rack, grill pan or elevated cooking rack. With the divisible baskets you can cook several things at once. It is impressive to see that a unit can cook so many things in so many ways.

Depending on the size of your fryer you can buy many accessories. Cake and pizza pans, kebab skewers and steamer are just some of the accessories I've seen.

4. Space saver

If you have a small kitchen or live in a dorm or shared apartment, you can appreciate this benefit. Most of these units are about the size of a coffee machine. They do not take up too much space on the counter and are generally easy to store or move.

I appreciate the fact that they can replace other appliances like a toaster and some people use them in kitchens in place of ovens.

5. Ease of use

Most fryers are very easy to use. Just choose the temperature and cooking time, add food and shake several times during cooking.

With the baskets you can shake your food easily and quickly and the device does not lose much heat when opened. So do not hesitate to check out if you want! Unlike an oven, you will not slow things down when you do it.

6. Easy cleaning

Part of the cooking that most of us do not appreciate is the cleaning. With an air fryer, you only have one basket and one pan to clean, and you can also use dishwasher. With non-stick coated parts, food does not normally stick to the pan. It only takes a few minutes to wash after use. It inspires me to cook more often at home, because I'm not afraid to clean!

7. Energy efficiency

These fryers are more efficient than using an oven. I used mine during a heat wave and I love that my kitchen is not hot when I use it. If you're trying to keep your home cool in the summer or worry about your electricity bills, you'll be impressed with the efficiency of these devices.

Who can benefit the most from an air fryer?

Everyone can benefit from using an air fryer but this is especially good for some groups.

Busy parents

Need a quick snack after school? Late, but the kids ask for dinner? Just throw chips and nuggets in one of these dishes and prepare dinner in about 15 minutes! Parents love the speed with which they prepare food and the ease with which they have to clean up. It takes less time than getting a pizza!

Seniors

This is a great option for seniors who just do not want to keep a hot stove or prepare many ingredients. You can use frozen meat, pre-cut vegetables and seasonal dishes to your liking. They are so easy to use and will not tire your hands and can do anything from snacks to a full meal. Easy to clean.

Students

The ultimate snack! If it's one o'clock in the morning and you're writing an article, just throw wings or chips or make a grilled sandwich. With an Air Fryer, you can become the most popular person in your dorm. Do not worry about the time that mess hall will close.

Easy

It can be difficult to be motivated to cook when living alone. It's just not worth heating the oven or spending a lot of time cutting things just to eat something. With a fryer you can prepare a small amount of food for a single serving in just a few minutes. Eat healthier and save money by not eating all the time! A Air Fryer is much more useful than a microwave and allows a lot of tasty food.

People who hate cooking

This is the ideal device for those who do not like to cook. You do not have to waste time, preparing ingredients for your food. You can use it with frozen meats like chicken wings, rib eye steaks and even frozen pizza. Make fries, onion rings, potatoes and nuggets in a few minutes. You can take a pack of pre-cut vegetables and make a quick stir fry. Grilled cheese sandwich sounds good? Go for it. Easy to use and clean, this fryer will not make you hate the kitchen.

Should I consider a fryer?

If you are fascinated by the benefits I mentioned, consider air frying. Perfect for small kitchens, dorms and offices, they enable you to prepare healthy meals quickly and easily. There are units of all sizes, from singles to large families, and they usually cost between $ 60 and $ 400. You can find the perfect device for your needs and cook the same evening.

How to preheat Air fryer?

A step-by-step guide and a few things to keep in mind:

1. Check the manual

The very first thing to do with any kind of electronic product is to read the manual. This also applies to a fryer. That way, you know exactly how to use the device, so you do not make mistakes or damage it.

This is very important for preheating, as some manufacturers may have their own preferred methods for this task. It is best to follow the instructions of these companies so that you do not cancel your warranty just because you want to use your new device.

2. Check the air fryer for cleanliness

Now that you know whether the manufacturer of your Air fryer has specific pre-heating instructions or not, the next step is to check the cleanliness of your device.

You need to be careful, as food remnants and debris can affect the taste of the next dish that you will prepare in the Air Fryer.

The basket must be thoroughly cleaned and properly dried before use. Check every angle of your cooking basket to make sure nothing is left.

3. Connect the device

As an electrical appliance, your Air Fryer must be connected in order to be used. Be careful, because not all fryers are equipped with a dual power supply.

If you are using a fryer that has been purchased in another country in the United States, check the voltage used by your location. The 120V appliances are grilled in a 220V outlet and nobody wants them. Always make sure first before connecting anything.

4. Put the accessories in place

If you want to use an accessory for your fryer, it is best to put it in the appliance before preheating. Therefore, the accessories can also be prepared for cooking. It will also make things easier if you do this step now.

If the fryer is already hot, you might not have ample grasp on it to place accessories securely. It is advisable to prepare the device at this point so that you do not have any problems later.

5. Turn on the device

The next step is pretty obvious: turn on your Air Fryer. Without the unit that is ready and willing to go, no magic will be performed. Once you have read the manual, you need to know where the power switch is located. Just tap it and you're ready to preheat.

6. Set the timer

Now, when the device is on, you can preheat it. The next step would be to set the timer. Experts say preheating should take more than three minutes. Preheating is generally recommended for 5 minutes, although it may depend on the unit you own.

Some units with pre-heating instructions have their own note for the preheating time of the fryers. Refer to this information and you will not go wrong.

7. Select the highest temperature settings

Although the duration may vary from device to device, the temperature settings are completely different. Almost all manufacturers will tell you that you must set the appliance to the highest heat setting for preheating.

It may seem exaggerated, but in reality, it works very well. This will allow your fryer to reach the desired temperature in minutes, so follow this step.

When the timer has expired, you have finished preheating. You can now load the food and start cooking.

8. Don't have time? Add 3 minutes to your cooking time instead

As mentioned above, some fryers do not require preheating. You can do that as well but with most prescriptions based on pre-heating times, this can discourage your cooking time.

To compensate for this, you can add 3 minutes to the timer setting for your recipe. In this way your ingredients are always cooked thoroughly and evenly.

If you think you do not want to preheat your fryer, you should also be prepared to make estimates and experiment.

You may need to check the doneness of your food several times before you reach the beautiful golden brown desired. A little patience may also be necessary if you ignore the preheating.

Final judgment

Even if you've never tried to work with an oven before, you do not have to worry about preheating your fryer.

The latter is a very basic cooking appliance, so you can be sure that preheating is not too difficult. You just have to know exactly what to do to get the job done.

Learning how to preheat the fryer takes just a few minutes of your time. However, it can bring fried, crispy and crunchy foods for a lifetime, so it's definitely worth it.

Air Fryer Fish and Fries

Ingredients

- 1 pound of potatoes (about 2 medium)
- 2 tablespoons olive oil
- 1/4 teaspoon pepper
- 1/4 teaspoon salt
- 1/3 cup all-purpose flour
- 1/4 teaspoon pepper
- 1 big egg
- 2 tablespoons of water
- 2/3 cup crushed cornflakes
- 1 tablespoon of grated Parmesan
- 1/8 teaspoon cayenne pepper
- 1/4 teaspoon salt
- Haddock or cod fillets

COOKING METHOD:

1. Preheat the fryer to 400 ° C.
2. Peel the potatoes and cut into 1/2-inch-thick slices.
3. Cut the slices into fries shape.
4. In a large bowl, mix the potatoes with oil, pepper and salt.
5. If necessary, work in several batches, place the potatoes in a single layer in the basket of the fryer. Cook for 5 to 10 minutes.
6. Mix the potatoes in the basket to redistribute them. Cook for 5 to 10 minutes until lightly browned and crispy.
7. In a shallow bowl mix flour and pepper.
8. In another shallow bowl, beat the egg.
9. In a third bowl mix the cornflakes with cheese and cayenne pepper.
10. Sprinkle the fish with salt; Dip in the flour mixture to cover both sides. Shake off the excess.
11. Dip into the egg mixture, then into the mixture of cornflakes, tap to make the coating stick.
12. Take the chips out of the basket.
13. Keep the fish in a single layer in the basket of the Air Fryer.
14. Cook until the fish is lightly browned and starts to loosen easily with a fork; Do not cook for too long.
15. Put the French fries back in the basket to keep them warm.
16. Serve immediately.

Air Fryer Spicy Barbecue Drumsticks

4 servings, preparation time 25 minutes, cooking time: 20 minutes.

Ingredients

- 1 clove of garlic
- ½ tablespoon mustard
- 2 teaspoons brown sugar
- 1 teaspoon of chilli powder
- Freshly ground black pepper
- 1 tablespoon of olive oil
- 4 Drumsticks

COOKING METHOD:

1. Preheat air fryer to 200 ° C
2. Mix the garlic with mustard, brown sugar, chilli powder, a pinch of salt and freshly ground pepper. Mix with the oil.

3. Rub the drumsticks thoroughly with the marinade and leave to marinate for 20 minutes.

4. Put the drumsticks in the basket and slide them into the air fryer.

5. Set the timer to 10 minutes.

6. Fry the drumsticks until golden brown.

7. Then lower the temperature to 150 ° C and cook the drumsticks for another 10 minutes.

8. Serve.

Air Fryer Roasted Lamb Rack

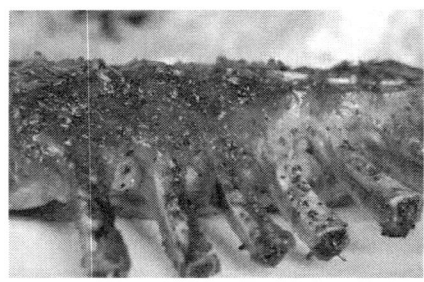

4 servings, preparation time 10 minutes, cooking time: 30 minutes.

Ingredients

- 1 clove of garlic
- 1 tablespoon of olive oil
- 800 g of lamb
- pepper and salt
- 75 g of unsalted macadamia nuts
- 1 tablespoon of breadcrumbs
- 1 tablespoon of chopped fresh rosemary
- 1 egg

COOKING METHOD:

1. Finely chop the garlic.
2. Mix the olive oil and garlic to get the garlic oil.
3. Brush the lamb with the oil and season with pepper and salt.
4. Preheat Air fryer to 100 ° C
5. Finely chop the nuts and place in a bowl.
6. Add the breadcrumbs and rosemary.
7. Beat egg in another bowl.
8. To cover the lamb, dip the meat into the egg mixture.
9. Cover the lamb with the macadamia crust.
10. Place the coated lamb rib in the air fryer basket and slide it into the air fryer.
11. Set the timer to 25 minutes.
12. Increase the temperature to 200 ° C after 25 minutes and set the timer for another 5 minutes.
13. Remove the meat and leave aside for 10 minutes covered with aluminum foil before serving.

Air Fryer Hot Fried Shrimps

4 servings, preparation time 10 minutes, cooking time: 6 minutes

Ingredients

- 1 tablespoon of chilli flakes
- 1 tablespoon chili powder
- ½ c. In the sea salt tea
- ½ c. Freshly ground black pepper
- 8-12 fresh prawns
- 3 tablespoons mayonnaise
- 1 tablespoon of tomato sauce
- 1 tablespoon of apple cider vinegar or wine

COOKING METHOD:

1. Preheat Air fryer to 180°C.
2. Mix the spices in a bowl.
3. Add the shrimp and mix well with the spices.
4. Put the spicy shrimp in the Air fryer basket.
5. Slide the basket into the Air Fryer and set the timer to between 6 and 8 minutes, depending on the size of the shrimp.
6. Serve the hot shrimp with sauce.

Air Fryer Chicken Breast

8 servings, preparation time 25+ minutes, cooking time: 20 minutes/batch

Ingredients

- 2 cups of buttermilk
- 2 tablespoons of Dijon mustard
- 2 teaspoons salt
- 2 teaspoons of spicy sauce
- 2 teaspoons of garlic powder
- 8 chicken halves with bone, without skin (8 ounces each)
- 2 cups bread crumbs
- 1 cup cornmeal
- 2 tablespoons rapeseed oil
- 1/2 teaspoon spice
- 1/2 teaspoon ground mustard

- 1/2 teaspoon paprika
- 1/2 teaspoon cayenne pepper
- 1/4 teaspoon dried oregano
- 1/4 teaspoon dried parsley flakes

COOKING METHOD:

1. Preheat the fryer to 375 ° C.
2. Combine the first five ingredients in a large bowl for making a marinade.
3. Add the chicken and marinate it with the marinade. Let it aside for 1 hour or overnight.
4. Mix the remaining ingredients in a shallow bowl and mix.
5. Add the chicken piece by piece and cover well again.
6. Place in the basket of the fryer with cooking spray in a single layer.
7. Fry in the air fryer until the thermometer indicates 170° and turns halfway, about 20 minutes.
8. Repeat this with the rest of the chicken.
9. When the last serving of chicken is cooked, put all the chicken back in the basket and fry it in the air for two or three minutes to keep it warm.

Air Fryer Chicken Strips

4 servings, preparation time 10 minutes, cooking time: 15 minutes/batch

Ingredients

- 1 whole bagel, torn
- 1/2 cup Panko bread crumbs (Japanese)
- 1/2 cup grated Parmesan
- 1/4 teaspoon chopped peppers
- 1/4 cup butter, diced
- A pound of chicken fillets
- 1/2 teaspoon salt

COOKING METHOD:

1. Preheat the fryer to 400 ° C.

2. Beat the broken bagel in a food processor until crumbs form.

3. Put 1/2 cup of breadcrumbs in a shallow bowl; Mix with panko, cheese and chilli flakes. (Discard or store the remaining bagel crumbs for another use).

4. Microwave the butter in a small microwave-proof bowl until it melts.

5. Sprinkle chicken with salt.

6. Dip in hot butter and add the mixture of breadcrumbs.

7. Spray the frying basket with a kitchen spray.

8. Put the chicken in a single layer in the frying basket.

9. If necessary, work in batch, cook for 7 minutes; bring the chicken back to the cook until the layer is browned, and the chicken is no longer pink for 7 to 8 minutes.

10. Serve immediately.

Air Fryer Stuffed Cheese Burger

4 servings, preparation: 20 min. Cooking time: 20 min / batch

Ingredients

- 1/4 cup diced cheddar cheese
- 2 green onions, chopped
- 2 tablespoons chopped fresh parsley
- 3 teaspoons of Dijon mustard, split
- 3 tablespoons dry bread crumbs
- 2 tablespoons ketchup
- 1/2 teaspoon salt
- 1/2 teaspoon dried rosemary, crushed
- 1/4 teaspoon dried salvia leaves
- 1 pound of lean ground beef (90% lean)

- 4 hamburger rolls, divided

COOKING METHOD:

1. Preheat the fryer to 375°C.

2. Mix cheddar cheese, spring onions, parsley and 1 teaspoon of mustard in a small bowl.

3. In another bowl, combine the breadcrumbs, ketchup, spices, and the remaining mustard.

4. Add the meat to the breadcrumb mixture; Mix lightly but thoroughly.

5. Make eight thin patties from the mixture.

6. Place the cheese mixture in the middle of every two patties.

7. Cover the remaining patties, tighten the edges, and make sure they are completely sealed making the two patties one.

8. Place the patties in a single layer in the frying basket.

9. Work in batch as needed, fry for 10 minutes in the air. Turnover and continue cooking until the thermometer indicates 160°C, ie another 8 to 10 minutes.

Air Fryer Meatballs

24 small meatballs, preparation: 20 min. Cooking time: 10 min / batch

Ingredients

- 2 tablespoons olive oil
- 4 garlic cloves, chopped
- 1 teaspoon curry powder
- 1 big egg slightly beaten
- 1 glass (4 ounces) of chopped peppers, drained
- 1/4 cup crumbs
- 1/4 cup chopped fresh parsley
- 1 tablespoon of chopped fresh rosemary
- 2 pounds of loose pork sausage(shredded)

COOKING METHOD:

1. Preheat the fryer to 200°C.//
2. Heat the oil over medium heat in a small pan.
3. Sauté the garlic with curry powder for 1 to 2 minutes.
4. Let it cool down a bit.
5. Mix egg, chili, breadcrumbs, parsley, rosemary and garlic in a bowl.
6. Add the sausages; Mix lightly but thoroughly.
7. Form into balls.
8. Place in a single layer in the frying basket.
9. Cook for 7 to 10 minutes until lightly browned and cooked.
10. Serve.

Air Fryer Avocado fries

4 servings, preparation: 15 min. Cooking time: 30 min

Ingredients

- 1/2 cup all-purpose flour
- 1 1/2 teaspoons of black pepper
- 2 eggs
- 1 tablespoon of water
- 1/2 cup panko (Japanese breadcrumbs)
- 2 avocados, each divided into 8 slices
- Cooking spray
- 1/4 teaspoon kosher salt
- 1/4 cup ketchup without added salt
- 2 tablespoons of canola mayonnaise
- 1 tablespoon of apple cider vinegar
- 1 tablespoon chilli sauce

COOKING METHOD:

1. Mix the flour and pepper in a bowl.

2. Beat eggs and water gently in a second bowl.

3. Put the panko in a third bowl.

4. Sprinkle the avocado in the flour.

5. Immerse the egg mixture and allow excess water to drip off.

6. Dredge in Panko, press to stick.

7. Coat avocado wedges well with cooking spray.

9. Place the avocado wedges in the air fryer and cook at 200°C until golden, 7 to 8 minutes, turning avocado half way.

10. Remove from the air fryer; sprinkle with salt.

11. While the fries are cooking stir ketchup, mayonnaise, vinegar and sriracha in a small bowl.

12. Serve with sauce.

Air Fryer Manchurian Cauliflower

2 Servings

Ingredients

- 1 tablespoon canola oil
- 2 tablespoon chopped garlic
- 2 tablespoon chopped ginger
- 1 small red onion diced
- 3 chopped scallions
- 2/3 cup vegetable broth, plus a little more if needed
- 1/3 cup sambal
- 1/2 cup of AP flour
- Corn starch 1/2 cup, plus 1-4 Tablespoon extra
- 2 teaspoon Onion powder
- 2 teaspoon of garlic powder
- 1 teaspoon garam masala

- 1 teaspoon of salt
- 1/2 teaspoon black pepper
- 1/2 teaspoon turmeric
- 1/2 cup of water
- 1 small cauliflower head cut into small pieces
- Canola, grapeseed or vegetable oil, for frying
- 2 servings of basmati rice prepared
- chopped cilantro for garnish

COOKING METHOD:

Sauce

1. Heat the oil in a medium saucepan over medium heat. Add garlic and ginger and sauté until soft, but not browned (about 7 minutes).

2. Add the red onions and scallions and mix. Add liquid to the pan as needed to soften the vegetables but not turn brown (10-15 minutes).

3. At this point, the vegetables should be soft and most of the liquid absorbed. Remove from heat and stir in the desired amount of sambal. Put aside.

Batter

1. Combine all batter ingredients in a medium bowl, except cornstarch and water.

2. Add water, stir gently and add one extra corn starch with one tablespoon after the other to get a smooth consistency. You want it to be thin enough to cover the cauliflower florets, but not too thin that it drips too fast or too thick that it doesn't cover florets evenly.

Cauliflower

1. Put the florets in a large pot. Cover with water and put a lid on it. Bring to a boil, then remove from heat and drain. Transfer them to a baking tray with a refrigerated shelf to allow the cauliflower to cool.

2. Add a few inches of oil to Air Fryer basket and heat to 175C.

3. Add several florets to the batter and carefully add one after the other to the hot oil. Fry till golden, then transfer to paper towels with a skimmer to drain, as you repeat the process with the rest of the florets. Do not overload the pot or your florets will stick together.

4. Mix the fried florets into the prepared sauce, then place in an air fryer at 200C for 8 to 10 minutes and shake them every few minutes to avoid sticking. (Depending on the size of your air fryer, you may need to do this in 2 to 4 batches.)

5. Serve immediately with prepared basmati rice and chopped cilantro.

Air Fryer Bourbon Bacon Burgers

Ingredients

- 1 tablespoon of bourbon
- 2 tablespoons of brown sugar
- 3 pieces of maple bacon halved
- ¾ lbs beef
- 1 tablespoon of chopped onion
- 2 tablespoons barbecue sauce
- ½ teaspoon salt
- freshly ground black pepper
- 2 slices of Colby Jack cheese (or Jack Monterey)
- 2 Kaiser rolls
- Tomato and lettuce for serving
- 2 tablespoons barbecue sauce
- 2 tablespoons mayonnaise

- ¼ teaspoon ground paprika

- Freshly ground black pepper

COOKING METHOD:

1. Preheat the fryer to 200°C and pour some water into the bottom of the fryer. (This prevents the grease that drops in the bottom drawer from burning and smoking.)

2. Mix bourbon and brown sugar in a small bowl. Put the bacon strips in the air fryer basket and brush with the brown sugar mix.

3. Air fry at 200 °C for 4 minutes. Turn the bacon over, sprinkle with brown sugar and air fry for another 4 minutes at 190°C until crispy.

4. While the bacon is cooking, prepare the burger patties.

5. In a large bowl, mix ground beef, onion, barbecue sauce, salt and pepper.

6. Gently mix with your hands and shape the meat into 2 patties.

7. Place the hamburger patties in the air fryer basket and fry the burgers at 180°C for 15 to 20 minutes, depending on how you like your burger (15 minutes for rare to medium).

8. While the burgers are air frying, prepare the burger sauce by combining the BBQ sauce, mayonnaise, paprika, and freshly ground black pepper to taste in a bowl.

9. When the burgers are cooked to your taste, top up patty with a slice of Colby Jack cheese and air fry for another minute just to melt the cheese. (You can attach the cheese slice to the burger with a toothpick to prevent it from being blown into the fryer.)

10. Put the sauce inside the buns, place the burgers patty on the buns and garnish with the bacon, salad and tomatoes and enjoy!

Air fryer Simple French Fries

2 Servings

Ingredients

- 2 medium potatoes (cut into about 1-inch pieces)
- Oil spray
- Pinch of salt and pepper
- 1 small pepper, medium hard
- 1 small onion, chopped medium

COOKING METHOD:

1. Put the potatoes in the basket of the fryer.

2. Spray with oil, shake, spray again and add a pinch of salt.

3. Set the air fryer to 200°C for ten minutes. Stop once to shake during the cooking time. (Do not hesitate to move if the potatoes are not moving enough)

4. After the potatoes have cooked for 10 minutes, add the peppers and onions.

5. Add another spray of oil and shake the basket. Set the air fryer to 200°C and cook for 15 minutes.

6. Check during the last 5 minutes that the potatoes are not too brown.

7. Depending on the size of your potatoes, you may need a little less time or a little more time.

8. If necessary, add a few extra minutes to the cooking time.

9. Add salt to taste and serve.

Air fryer Hot Dogs

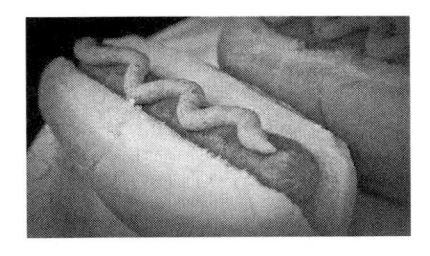

2 servings, preparation: 3 min. Cooking time: 10 minutes.

Ingredients

- 2 hot dogs sausage
- 2 hot dog rolls
- 2 tablespoons of grated cheese, if desired

COOKING METHOD:

1. Preheat your Air Fryer to 180°C for about 4 minutes.
2. Put two sausages in the Air Fryer and cook for about 5 minutes.
3. Take the sausage out of the Air Fryer.
4. Put it into a bun, add cheese if desired.
5. Serve.

Air Fryer Hot chicken

4 Servings

Ingredients

- 1 chicken with 4 pounds, cut into 6 pieces (2 breasts, 2 thighs and 2 mortars)
- 2 eggs
- 1 cup buttermilk
- 2 cups of flour for all purposes
- 2 tablespoons of paprika
- 1 teaspoon of garlic powder
- 1 teaspoon of onion powder
- 2 teaspoons salt
- 1 teaspoon freshly ground black pepper
- vegetable oil

Nashville hot sauce:

- 1 tablespoon of cayenne pepper
- 1 teaspoon salt
- ¼ cup vegetable oil
- 4 slices of white bread
- Cucumbers with dill

COOKING METHOD:

1. Cut the chicken breast into two pieces for a total of 8 pieces of chicken.
2. Beat eggs and buttermilk in a bowl.
3. Combine flour, paprika, garlic powder, onion powder, salt and black pepper in a plastic bag with zipper.
4. Dip the chicken pieces into the egg-butter mixture and mix with the seasoned flour, covering all sides.
5. Repeat this process (egg mixture and then flour mixture) again.
6. Make sure all sides of the chicken are completely covered.
7. Sprinkle chicken with vegetable oil and put aside.
8. Preheat the fryer to 200°C. Spray or brush the bottom of the frying basket with some vegetable oil.
9. Roast the chicken in two courses at 180°C for 20 minutes and turn the pieces in half (check in between time depends on size).

10. Transfer the chicken to a plate, but do not cover it. Repeat this with the second batch of chicken.

11. Reduce the frying temperature to 100°C. Place the first batch of chicken with the second batch already in the basket and fry for another 7 minutes.

12. While the chicken is roasting in the air fryer, mix cayenne and salt in a bowl.

13. Heat the vegetable oil in a small saucepan.

14. When it is very hot, add it to the spice mixture with stirring until smooth.

15. It will sizzle briefly when added to spices.

16. Put the fried chicken on the slices of white bread and coat the chicken with the spicy sauce.

17. Serve hot.

Air Fryer Lemon cookies

Ingredients

- 1/2 cup unsalted butter softened
- 1 pack (3.4 oz.) Instant Lemon Pudding Mix
- 1/2 cup of sugar
- 1 big egg
- 2 tablespoons milk 2%
- 1-1 / 2 cup all-purpose flour
- 1 teaspoon baking soda
- 1/4 teaspoon salt

Icing:

- 2/3 cup powdered sugar
- 2 to 4 teaspoons of lemon juice

COOKING METHOD:

1. In a large bowl, stir butter, pudding mix and sugar. Beat in egg and the milk.

2. Add flour, baking powder and salt in cream mixture and beat them properly.

3. Divide the dough in half. Form a 6 "inch long roll on a lightly floured surface, wrap and refrigerate for 3 hours.

4. Preheat the Air fryer to 162°C. Unwrap the dough and cut it crossways into 1/2 inches. Place the slices in a single layer in an air fryer basket.

5. Fry until the edges are light brown, 8-12 minutes.

6. Let it rest in the basket for 2 minutes. Repeat with the remaining dough.

7. Mix the sugar and lemon juice in a small bowl.

8. Serve

Air Fryer Thanksgiving Turkey

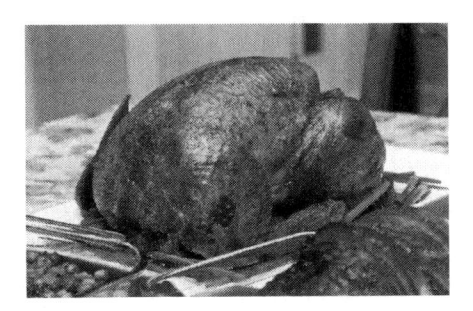

4 servings

Ingredients

- 1 turkey breast (2 pounds)
- Kosher salt
- Freshly ground black pepper
- 1 tablespoon of freshly chopped thyme
- 1 tablespoon of freshly chopped rosemary tea
- 1 tablespoon of freshly chopped salad
- 1/4 c. maple syrup
- 2 tablespoons of Dijon mustard
- 1 tablespoon of melted butter

COOKING METHOD:

1. Season the turkey breast with salt and pepper and sprinkle with fresh herbs.

2. Place in a Air fryer and fry at 187° C for 30 to 35 minutes or until the internal temperature reaches 120° C.

3. In a small bowl, mix maple syrup, Dijon and melted butter.

4. Remove the turkey from the Air Fryer and brush off the mixture.

5. Roast and fry at 160°C until caramelization, 2 minutes.

6. Leave for 15 minutes before cutting.

Air Fryer Jalapeno Poppers

Ingredients

- 10 jalapeno peppers halved
- 8 ounces of cream cheese
- 1/4 cup fresh parsley
- Gluten-free tortilla 3/4 c or breadcrumbs

COOKING METHOD:

1. Mix half of the crumbs and cream cheese together. Once combined, add the parsley.

2. Fill each pepper with this mixture.

3. Gently squeeze the top of the peppers into the remaining 1/4 c crumbs to create the top layer.

4. Cook in air fryer at 187°C for 6 to 8 minutes.

5. Let cool and enjoy!

Air Fryer Cinnamon Rolls

Ingredients

1 pound of bread dough, thawed

¼ cup melted and cooled butter

Brown sugar bowl

1 ½ tablespoons of cinnamon powder

4 ounces of cream cheese,

2 tablespoons soft butter

1 ¼ cup powdered sugar

½ teaspoon of vanilla

COOKING METHOD:

1. Let the bread dough at the counter come back to room temperature. Roll the dough into a rectangle (13 "x 11") on a lightly floured surface.

2. Position the rectangle so that the 13-inch side faces you.

3. Brush the melted butter over the dough and leave a 1-inch edge at its outermost edge.

4. Mix the brown sugar and cinnamon in a small bowl.

5. Sprinkle the mixture evenly over the dough with butter and leave the 1-inch edge free.

6. Roll the dough tightly.

7. Cut the stem into 8 pieces, cut slowly with a cutting motion to avoid flattening the dough.

8. Let the rolls rest for 1 ½ to 2 hours.

9. For frosting, place the cream cheese and butter in a microwave-proof container.

10. Soften the mixture in the microwave for 30 seconds until it is easy to stir. Slowly add the powdered sugar and mix. Add the vanilla extract and stir until smooth.

11. When the rollers are up, preheat the Air Fryer to 180°C.

12. Put 4 rolls in the frying basket.

13. Fry for 5 minutes in the air.

14. Turn the rolls and fry again for 4 minutes.

15. Repeat this with the remaining 4 rolls.

16. Let the buns cool for a few minutes before icing them.

17. Distribute large quantities of cream cheese on hot cinnamon rolls.

18. Serve hot and enjoy!

Air Fryer Kofta Kebab

4 servings, preparation time 10 minutes, cooking time: 20 minutes

Ingredients

- 1 tablespoon of oil
- 1 pound of 85% ground beef
- ¼ cup of chopped parsley
- 1 tablespoon of chopped garlic
- 2 tablespoons Kofta Kabab Mix
- 1 teaspoon salt

COOKING METHOD:

1. Mix all ingredients with a blender.

2. If you have time, let the mixture stand in the fridge for 30 minutes.

3. You can also mix and reserve for a day or two until you are ready to do the Kababs.

4. Divide the meat into four pieces and make four long sausage shapes.

5. Put the kebabs in your air fryer and cook for 10 minutes at 45°C.

6. Sprinkle with parsley and serve with tomato salad with cucumber and pita bread.

Air Fryer Peach Pies

4 servings, preparation time 10 minutes, cooking time: 20 minutes

Ingredients

- 2 fresh peaches (5 ounces), peeled and chopped
- 1 tablespoon of fresh lemon juice (of 1 lemon)
- 3 tablespoons of sugar
- 1 teaspoon of vanilla extract
- 1/4 teaspoon of table salt
- 1 teaspoon corn-starch
- 1 pkg (14.1 oz) pie crust
- Cooking spray

COOKING METHOD:

1. Mix peaches, lemon juice, sugar, vanilla and salt in a medium bowl.

2. Let rest for 15 minutes and stir occasionally. Drain peaches, reserving 1 tablespoon of liquid.

3. Stir corn starch into the reserved liquid; stir into drained peaches.

4. Cut the piecrust into 8 (4-inch circles).

5. Put about 1 tablespoon of stuffing in the middle of each circle.

6. Coat the edges of the dough with water.

7. Fold the dough over the filling to form half-moon.

8. Crimp the edges with a fork to seal; Cut 3 small slits into the top of the pies.

9. Cover the pies well with a cooking spray.

10. Place 3 pies in a single layer in the frying basket and fry at 176°C until golden, 12 to 14 minutes.

11. Repeat with the other pies.

Air Fryer Parchment Paper Fish

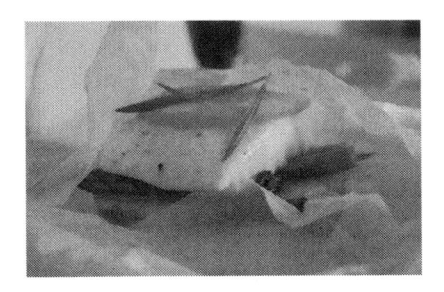

4 servings, preparation time 10 minutes, cooking time: 15 minutes

Ingredients

- 2 thawed cod fillets
- 1/2 cup carrots julienne
- 1/2 cup fennel tubers in julienne or 1/4 cup celery julienne
- 1/2 cup chopped red paprika
- 2 tarragon sticks or 1/2 teaspoon dried tarragon
- 2 carrots of melted butter
- 1 tablespoon of lemon juice
- 1 tablespoon divided salt
- 1/2 teaspoon pepper
- 1 tablespoon of oil

COOKING METHOD:

1. Combine melted butter, tarragon, 1/2 teaspoon salt and lemon juice in a medium bowl. Mix well until you get a creamy sauce.

2. Add the julienne vegetables and mix well. skip

3. Cut out two parchment squares big enough to cover fish and vegetables.

4. Sprinkle the fish fillets on both sides of the fillets with oil, salt and pepper.

5. Spread a net over each parchment square. Garnish each with half of the vegetables. Pour the rest of the sauce over the vegetables.

6. Fold the parchment paper and squeeze the sides to keep the fish, vegetables and sauce in the pack.

7. Put the packs in the air fryer basket.

8. Put your air fryer at 180°C for 15 minutes. Remove each pack on a plate and open it just before serving.

Air Fryer Asparagus Fried

2 servings, preparation time 5 minutes, cooking time: 10 minutes

Ingredients

1/2 bunch of asparagus, the lower part cut

Avocado or olive oil in a mister or sprayer.

Salt

Black pepper

COOKING METHOD:

1. Place the asparagus spears in the basket of the air fryer.
2. Lightly rub with oil, then sprinkle with salt and a little black pepper.
3. Place the basket in the fryer and cook for 10 minutes at 180°C.
4. Serve immediately.

Air Fryer Beetroot Chips

Even if you hate beetroot, try it!! You will love these beet chips.

2 servings, preparation time 5 minutes, cooking time: 15 minutes

Ingredients

- 2 medium-sized beetroot
- 1/2 teaspoon of oil
- salt to taste
- Pepper optional

COOKING METHOD:

1. Wash beetroot, peel and remove skin.

2. Cut into thin slices with a mandolin cutter.

3. Otherwise, if you do not have a cutting machine, cut it evenly with your knife.

4. Use the skin to dye your accessories if you wish or dispose of them in your food waste.

5. Divide the beet slices onto the paper and place another piece of paper on top.

6. Keep it aside for 10 minutes. This process absorbs extra moisture on the turnips.

7. Sprinkle the necessary salt on the beets.

8. Preheat the Air fryer to 150°C for 4 minutes.

9. Remove the basket from the air fryer and put the chips in it.

10. Slide it into the air fryer and fry for 15 minutes.

11. Be sure to remove and shake well every 5 minutes.

12. Once the fries are crispy on the outside edges and tender in the middle, let them cool for a while.

13. Slide the basket with the chips and heat for another 3 minutes at 180°C. The chips will be sharp and perfect.

14. If necessary, season with sea salt and freshly ground pepper or just snorkel on it.

Air Fryer Cauliflower Nuggets

2 servings, preparation time 5 minutes, cooking time: 15 minutes

Ingredients

- 1 large cauliflower head divided into small flowers
- 2 big eggs
- 1/4 cup coconut flour
- 1 tablespoon teaspoon of garlic powder
- 1 tablespoon of onion powder
- Spraying or mist of coconut oil
- 1 tablespoon of dried parsley
- Season with salt and pepper.

COOKING METHOD:

1. Separate the cauliflower into small florets.

2. Add 2 tablespoons of water to the florets in a large microwave-safe bowl.

3. Cover it with plastic wrap and microwaves for 3 to 5 minutes. The Flower should be tender but not pasty.

4. If it is done badly, heat it for a minute or two in the microwave. Drain well.

5. Combine the florets in a shredder or food processor and mix until they look like rice grains. Pour it into a bowl.

6. Add the beaten eggs, coconut flour, garlic powder, onion powder, dried parsley, salt and pepper. Mix well

7. Take a small amount of the mixture and give it the desired shape. Let the cauliflower cool for 30 minutes.

8. Generously grease the frying basket. Put the cauliflower in a layer and sprinkle with coconut oil or mist.

9. Fry for 12 minutes at 180°C in the air fryer.

10. Serve hot.

Air Fryer Taco Bell Wraps

2 servings, preparation time 5 minutes, cooking time: 15 minutes

Ingredients

- 2 pounds of ground beef
- 2 sachets of taco seasoning
- 1 1/3 cup of water
- 6 flour tortillas 12 inches
- 3 tomatoes Roma
- 12 ounces nacho cheese
- 2 cups shredded salad
- 2 cups Mexican cheese
- 2 cups sour cream
- 6 Tostadas
- Olive oil or butter spray

COOKING METHOD:

1. Preheat the fryer to 180°C.

2. Prepare meat according to tacos seasoning manual.

3. Fill the middle of each tortilla with 2/3 c beef, 4 tablespoons Nacho cheese, 1 Tostada, 1/3 c sour cream, 1/3 c salad. 1/6 c of tomatoes and 1/3 c of cheese

4. To close, flood the edges up, over the middle, this should look like a pinwheel.

5. Repeat with the remaining wraps.

6. Put the curved side in your fryer.

7. Spray with oil.

8. Cook for 2 minutes or until brown.

9. Carefully turn over with a spatula and spray.

10. Cook another 2 minutes and repeat with the other wraps.

Air Fryer Calzones

4 servings, preparation time 5 minutes, cooking time: 15 minutes

Ingredients

- 1 teaspoon of olive oil

- 1/4 cup finely chopped red onion (from 1 small onion)

- 3 ounces of spinach leaves (about 3 cups)

- 1/3 cup of sodium marinara sauce

- 2 ounces of grated chicken breast (about 1/3 cup)

- 6 ounces of freshly prepared whole wheat pizza dough

- 1 1/2 ounces pre-shredded mozzarella cheese (about 6 tablespoons)

- Cooking spray

COOKING METHOD:

1. Heat the oil in a medium to medium non-stick pan.
2. Add the onion and cook, stirring occasionally for 2 minutes.
3. Add the spinach; cover and cook until wilted for 1 1/2 minutes.
4. Remove the pan from the heat; stir marinara sauce and chicken.
5. Divide the dough into 4 equal pieces.
6. Roll each piece over a lightly floured surface in a 6-inch circle.
7. Add a quarter of the spinach mixture to half of each circle of dough.
8. Garnish each with a quarter of the cheese.
9. Fold the dough over the filling to form half-moons and squeeze the edges to seal them.
10. Coat the calzones well with a cooking spray.
11. Place the calzone in the frying basket and bake at 160°C until golden brown, after 8 minutes turn the calzone.
12. Cook total for 12-15 minutes.
13. Your Calzones are ready.

Air Fryer Pumpkin French Fries

2 Servings

Ingredients

- 250 g pumpkin
- 1 teaspoon of thyme
- 1 tablespoon of mustard
- Salt pepper
- Optional tomato sauce

COOKING METHOD:

1. Peel the pumpkin, remove the seeds and cut into pieces.
2. Put it in the Air fryer for 15 minutes at 198°C.
3. While cooking, stir and season with thyme, mustard, salt and pepper.
4. Serve hot with tomato sauce.

Air Fryer Whole Wheat Pizza

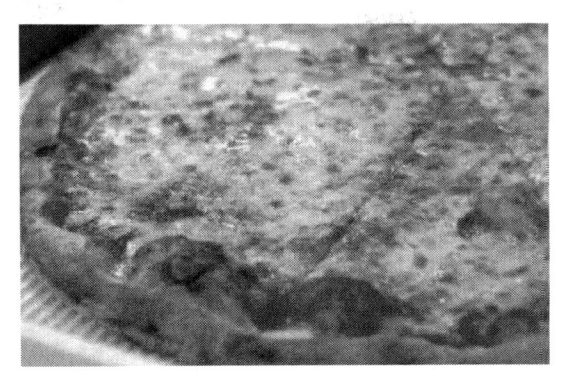

4 Servings

Ingredients

- 1/4 cup of sodium marinara sauce
- 2 whole wheat pita rounds
- 1 cup of spinach leaves (1 ounce)
- Cut 1 small tomato into 8 slices
- 1 small garlic clove chopped
- 1 oz partially sliced mozzarella cheese (about 1/4 cup)
- 1/4 oz Parmigiano-Reggiano cheese (about 1 tablespoon)

COOKING METHOD:

1. Distribute the marinara sauce evenly on one side of each pita bread.

2. Garnish with half the spinach leaves, sliced tomatoes, garlic and cheese.

3. Put 1 pita in the frying basket and bake at 176°C until the cheese melts and the pita is crispy, 4 to 5 minutes.

4. Repeat with the rest of the pita.

Air Fryer Lava Cakes with Peppermint

2 Servings

Ingredients

- 2/3 cup of semi-sweet pieces of chocolate
- 1/2 cup butter diced
- 1 cup icing sugar
- 2 big eggs
- 2 large egg yolks
- 1 teaspoon peppermint extract
- 6 tablespoons all-purpose flour
- 2 tablespoons finely ground mints, optional

COOKING METHOD:

1. Preheat the fryer to 190°C.

2. In a microwaveable bowl, melt the chocolate chips and butter for 30 seconds; stir until smooth.

3. Mix powdered sugar, eggs, egg yolks and extract until a smooth mixture is obtained.

4. Stir in the flour.

5. Generously grease and flour four, 4-oz. ramekins; pour the dough into the ramekins.

6. Do not overfill. Put the ramekins in the air fryer basket for 10 to 12 minutes. Do not overcook

7. Remove from the air fryer; Let stand for 5 minutes. Carefully roll a knife over the sides of the Ramekins several times to loosen the cake.

8. Invert onto the dessert plates. Sprinkle with crushed candies.

9. Serve immediately.

Air Fryer Wasabi Crab Cakes

2 servings, preparation: 5mins. Cooking time: 15 mins

Ingredients

- 1 medium red pepper finely chopped
- 1 celery rib finely chopped
- 3 green onions finely chopped
- 2 large egg whites
- 3 tablespoons lighter mayonnaise
- 1/4 teaspoon of prepared wasabi
- 1/4 teaspoon salt
- 1/3 cup plus 1/2 cup breadcrumbs, divided
- 1/ 2 cup crab in pieces, drained
- cooking spray

SAUCE:

- 1 chopped celery
- 1/3 cup light mayonnaise
- 1 chopped green onion
- 1 tablespoon of pleasure
- 1/2 teaspoon of wasabi
- 1/4 teaspoon of celery salt

COOKING METHOD:

1. Preheat the Air fryer to 190°C.

2. Spray fryer with cooking spray.

3. Combine the first seven ingredients; add 1/3 cup of bread crumbs.

4. Carefully stir in the crab.

5. Put the remaining breadcrumbs in a bowl.

6. Add crab mixture in the crumbs.

7. Coat and shape gently into 3/4 "thick pies, work in batches as needed and place the crab cakes in a single layer in a frying basket

8. Spritz crab cakes with boiling spray.

9. Cook for 8 to 12 minutes until golden, turning halfway through cooking.

10. Spray with additional cooking spray.

11. Remove and keep warm.

12. Repeat with the remaining crab cakes.

13. In the meantime, pour the ingredients of the sauce into the food processor; blend for two to three times to mix or until the desired consistency is achieved.

14. Serve the crab cakes immediately with the sauce.

Air Fryer Sweet Potato Fries

2 servings, preparation: 5mins. Cooking time: 15 min

Ingredients

- 2 medium sweet potatoes
- Half a tablespoon of coconut oil.
- 1 tablespoon of starch or corn-starch
- Optionally melted butter of 2 tbsp.
- Salt
- 1/4 cup coconut sugar or raw sugar
- 1 to 2 tablespoons cinnamon
- Optional powdered sugar for sprinkling

COOKING METHOD:

1. Peel the sweet potatoes, wash them with clean water and dry them.

2. Cut the peeled sweet potatoes 1/2 inch thick.

3. Mix the sweet potato slices in 1/2 teaspoon.

4. Put in the fryer at 190°C for 18 minutes. Give them a shake in halfway about 8-9 minutes.

5. Remove the fries from the Air Fryer and place them in a large bowl.

6. Sprinkle with 2 tbsp Butter on fries.

7. Then mix the cinnamon and the sugar and mix the fries again.

8. Put in a bowl and sprinkle with powdered sugar.

Air Fryer Roasted broccoli with cheese sauce

2 servings, preparation:5 min. Cooking time: 15 min

Ingredients

- 6 cups broccoli florets (about 12 ounces)
- Cooking spray
- 10 tablespoons low-fat condensed milk
- 1 1/2 oz queso fresco (fresh Mexican cheese), crumbled (about 5 tbsp)
- 4 teaspoons aj amarillo paste
- 6 crackers

COOKING METHOD:

1. Coat the broccoli florets well with cooking spray.

2. Place half of the broccoli in a frying basket and cook at 190°C until soft, 6 to 8 minutes.

3. Repeat the process with the remaining broccoli.

4. In the meantime, pour condensed milk, Queso Fresco, Ají Amarillo paste and salt into a blender; treat until smooth, about 45 seconds.

5. Put the sauce in a microwave-safe bowl. Microwave at maximum power for about 30 seconds.

6. Serve the cheese sauce with broccoli.

Air Fryer Turkey Breast

2 servings, preparation: 1day. Cooking time: 45 min

Ingredients

- 7 pounds of turkey breast

For the marinate:

- 1/2 cup salt
- 1 lemon
- 1/2 onion
- 3 crushed garlic cloves
- 5 sprigs of fresh thyme
- 3 bay leaves
- black pepper

For the turkey breast:

- 4 tbsp Unsalted butter on the table, softened.
- 1/2 tsp Black pepper
- 1/2 tsp Teaspoon of garlic powder
- 1/4 tsp Dry thyme
- 1/4 tsp Dry oregano

COOKING METHOD:

For the marinate:

1. Boil about 6 cups of water and add the salt.
2. Stir until the salt dissolves completely.
3. Allow to cool to room temperature.
4. Place the turkey breast in a large saucepan.
5. Put the rest of the brine ingredients with the turkey breast in the pan and cover with salt water.
6. Fill with fresh water until the turkey breast is completely submerged.

7   Cover the jar with plastic wrap and place in the refrigerator for 18 to 24 hours.

8   When you are ready to cook the bird, remove it from the pan and rinse with clear water. Dry with paper towels.

For the turkey breast:

1   In a bowl, mix the soft butter, the black pepper, the garlic powder, the thyme and the oregano to make a paste.

2   Pull gently on the skin of the breast and squeeze the butter between the breast and the skin.

3   If desired, season the outside of the breast with additional pepper and garlic powder.

4   Preheat your fryer for at least 5 minutes at 190°C.

5   Place the turkey breast with the breast down in the Air Fryer.

6   Cook for 45 minutes at 190°C.

7   Turn the turkey breast and cover the top of the breast with aluminum foil.

8   Continue for another 35 minutes at 190°C.

9   Remove the foil and cook for another 10 minutes until the turkey breast is browned and an instantly readable thermometer indicates 165°C in the thickest part of the breast.

10 Remove from the Air Fryer and lightly cover with foil for 10 to 15 minutes until sliced. Serve!

Air Fryer Brownies

Ingredients

DRY INGREDIENTS

- 1/2 cup of whole wheat flour
- 1/2 cup vegan sugar
- 1/4 cup cocoa powder
- 1 tablespoon of flaxseed
- 1/4 teaspoon salt

WET INGREDIENTS

- 1/4 cup non-dairy milk
- 1/4 cup of Aquafaba

- 1/2 teaspoon vanilla extract

    The additional ingredients

    One or a combination of the following:

Chopped nuts, hazelnuts, walnuts, mini vegan chocolate chips, grated coconut

COOKING METHOD:

1. Mix the dry ingredients in a bowl.
2. Then mix the wet ingredients in a large measuring cup.
3. Add the wet to dry and mix well.
4. Add the additional ingredients and mix again.
5. Preheat your fryer to 180°C.
6. Spray oil into a 5-inch cake pan or pie or cover with parchment paper to keep it oil-free.
7. Put the pan in the frying basket.
8. Cook for 20 minutes.
9. If the centre is not secure or a knife does not come out clean, if it gets stuck in the middle, cook for another 5 minutes and repeat if necessary.
10. The duration may vary depending on the size of the pan and Air Fryer.

Air Fryer Mexican Street Corn

2 Servings

Ingredients

- 4 corns peeled and cleaned.
- ¼ cup mayonnaise
- ½ teaspoon wide chili powder
- 1 lime, juice

Topping

- Cotija cheese, grated
- Limes
- Coriander, chopped

COOKING METHOD:

1. Put the 2 corn pieces in your air fryer and fry it in the air for 20-25 minutes until well cooked at 180°C.

2. Mix mayonnaise, chili and lemon juice.

3. Carefully remove the corn and apply the mayonnaise mixture on it.

4. Put the corn back in the Air Fryer and fry in the air for 2-3 minutes.

5. Use pliers to remove the corn and cover with cotija cheese.

6. Serve with lime slices and coriander.

Air Fryer Kale Crisp

Ingredients

- 1 bunch of Tuscan kale, stems and ribs removed, leaves cut into 5 cm pieces
- 2 tablespoons olive oil
- 1/2 tsp Kosher salt and more to taste.
- 1/4 tsp freshly ground pepper

COOKING METHOD:

1. Preheat a Philips Air Fryer to 195°C .
2. In a large bowl, mix the kale, olive oil and 1/2 teaspoon. salt and pepper

3. If you work batch wise, put the kale in the frying basket and place it in the Air Fryer.

4. Cook until the kale is crisp, about 5 minutes, and stir and shake the basket halfway during cooking.

5. Put the crisp in a bowl and season with salt. Serve hot or at room temperature.

Air Fryer Stuffed Peppers

Ingredients

- 2 peppers, stems and medium green seeds - boiled for 3 minutes in boiling salted water

- ½ medium onion, chopped

- 1 clove of garlic

- 1 teaspoon of olive oil

- ounces of lean ground beef

- ½ cup tomato sauce

- 1 teaspoon Worcestershire sauce

- ½ teaspoon salt

- ½ teaspoon black pepper

- Cheddar cheese 4 ounces, grated

COOKING METHOD:

1. Pre Heat the air fryer at 195°C.

2. Fry the onion and garlic in a small coated pan until golden brown and cool.

3. Combine beef, cooked vegetables, ¼ cup tomato sauce, Worcestershire, salt and pepper, and half the grated cheese in a medium bowl.

4. Divide the pepper halves and fill.

5. Add the rest of the tomato sauce and the cheese.

6. Put them in the frying basket and fry them in the air or bake until the meat is well cooked. - From 15 to 20 minutes.

Air Fryer Doughnuts

4 Servings

Ingredients

- 1/4 cup of warm water
- 1 teaspoon dry yeast 1/4 cup
- 1/2 cup powdered sugar
- 2 cups of flour for all purposes
- 1/4 teaspoon kosher salt
- 1/4 cup whole milk
- 2 tablespoons butter without salt
- 1 big egg
- 1 cup (about 4 ounces) powdered sugar
- 4 teaspoons tap water

COOKING METHOD:

1. Mix water, yeast and 1/2 teaspoon of granulated sugar in a small bowl.

2. Leave it for about 5 minutes.

3. Mix flour, salt and 1/4 cup of the remaining crystallized sugar in a medium bowl.

4. Add the yeast mixture, milk, butter and egg; Stir with a wooden spoon until a smooth dough is formed.

5. Place the dough on a lightly floured surface and knead until smooth for 1 to 2 minutes.

6. Transfer the dough to a lightly greased bowl. Cover and let rise in a warm place until the volume has doubled (about 1 hour).

7. Turn the dough onto a lightly floured surface. Gently wrap to a thickness of 1/4 inch.

8. Cut 8 donuts with a 3-inch circular cutter and a 1-inch circular cutter to remove the centre.

9. Place donuts and donut holes on a lightly floured surface.

10. Cover with plastic and allow to stand until the volume has doubled (about 30 minutes).

11. Place 2 donuts and 2 holes in a single layer in the frying basket and bake at 176°C until golden brown, 4 to 5 minutes.

12. Repeat this with the remaining donuts and holes.

13. Mix the icing sugar and tap water in a medium bowl until smooth.

14. Dip the donuts and donut holes in the enamel; Place it in a rack on a baking sheet to allow excessive frost to drain off.

15. Let the mixture stand for about 10 minutes until the enamel has solidified.

Air Fryer Chicken Popcorn

Ingredients

Marinate:

- 2 pounds of chicken breast fillets, cut into small pieces
- 2 cups almond milk
- 1 tsp salt tea
- 1/2 tsp Black pepper
- 1/2 ground paprika

Dry ingredients:

- 3 cups of flour
- 3 tsp salt tea
- 2 tablespoons of black pepper
- 2 tablespoons with paprika
- oil spray

COOKING METHOD:

1. Set aside three bowls.

2. Add chicken and marinade ingredients in a large zippered pocket.

3. Marinate in the fridge for at least 2 hours and for up to 6 hours.

4. Add the dry ingredients in a large, shallow bowl.

5. After marinating, place the chicken and marinade in a large bowl.

6. Mix the chicken parts in small portions with the dry ingredients, dip briefly into the marinade and coagulate them a second time in the dry ingredients that cover each chicken piece.

7. Spray olive oil on the bottom and sides of the inside of the frying container.

8. Put the breaded chicken in an even layer. Set the rest of the chicken aside. Sprinkle the top of the chicken quickly in the frying bowl with olive oil and place it in the Air Fryer.

9. Cook in the fryer at 180°C for 8 minutes; Shake half

10. Remove from the Air Fryer and repeat the steps until the chicken is done.

11. Serve immediately.

Air Fryer Fried Rice

Ingredients

- 2 cups cooked white rice
- 1 tablespoon of vegetable oil
- 2 teaspoons of sesame oil on the grill
- Kosher salt and freshly ground black pepper.
- 1 teaspoon Sriracha
- 1 teaspoon soy sauce
- 1/2 teaspoon sesame, preferably toast, more
- 1 big egg slightly beaten
- 1 cup of carrots and frozen peas, thawed

COOKING METHOD:

1. Mix rice, vegetable oil, 1 teaspoon of sesame oil and 1 tablespoon of water in a bowl.

2. Season with salt and pepper and mix to cover the rice.

3. Place the pan in an air fryer and cook at 175°C by half-stirring until the rice is lightly toasted and crisp, about 12 minutes.

4. In a small bowl mix the Sriracha, the soy sauce, the sesame seeds and the remaining oil of a teaspoon of sesame in a bowl.

5. Open the air fryer and pour the egg over the rice. Close and cook until the egg is cooked (about 4 minutes).

6. Open again, add the peas and carrots and add the rice to split and break the egg.

7. Close and cook for another 2 minutes to heat the peas and carrots.

8. Pour the fried rice into bowls, sprinkle with some sauce and sprinkle with more sesame seeds.

Air Fryer crispy onion

Ingredients

- 1/2 cup (about 2 1/8 oz)
- all-purpose flour
- 1 teaspoon smoked paprika
- 1/2 teaspoon kosher salt
- 1 big egg divided
- 1 tablespoon of water
- 1 cup breadcrumbs
- 1 onion (10 ounces) Cut into 1/2-inch-thick slices and separated into rings
- cooking spray
- 1/4 cup Greek yogurt 1% low fat

- 2 tablespoons of canola mayonnaise
- 1 tablespoon of tomato sauce
- 1 teaspoon Dijon
- Mustard 1/4 teaspoon
- garlic powder
- 1/4 teaspoon paprika

COOKING METHOD:

1. Mix flour, smoked paprika and 1/4 teaspoon salt in a shallow bowl.

2. Slightly beat the egg and water in a shallow second bowl.

3. Mix the breadcrumbs and the remaining teaspoon of salt in a shallow third bowl.

4. Sprinkle the onion rings into the flour mixture and remove the excess.

5. Dip the egg mixture and let the excess drip off.

6. Dredge into the breadcrumb's mixture.

7. Cover both sides of the onion rings thoroughly with a cooking spray.

8. Place the onion rings in a single layer in the frying basket and cook at 190°C until golden brown and crispy on both sides, 10 minutes, and turn the onion rings.

9. Cover warm while cooking the remaining onion rings.

10. Mix yogurt, mayonnaise, ketchup, mustard, garlic powder and paprika in a small bowl for the dip.

11. To serve, add 6 to 7 slices of onion to each plate with 2 tablespoons of sauce

Air Fryer Tofu Brown Rice

Ingredients

- Bag of 2 Tofu (14 oz) drained and diced
- cooking spray
- 1/4 cup natural orange juice (from 1 orange)
- 2 tablespoons low in sodium soy sauce
- 1+1 teaspoons of honey
- 1 teaspoon of sesame oil toasted
- 1 teaspoon rice vinegar
- 1/2 teaspoon corn-starch
- 1/2 cup cooked brown rice

- 1/2 teaspoon kosher salt

- 2 tablespoons of chopped shallots

- 1 tablespoon grilled sesame seeds

COOKING METHOD:

1. Preheat oven to 195°C

2. Place the tofu in a bowl covered with several layers of paper towels.

3. Cover with extra paper towels and a second bowl. Put a weight on the top. Leave for 30 minutes.

4. Cover the tofu with a cooking spray before putting in the air fryer basket.

5. Put half of the tofu in a single layer in the frying basket and cook at 190°C (about 15 minutes) until crisp and golden yellow.

6. Mix orange juice, soy sauce, honey, sesame oil, rice vinegar and corn-starch in a small saucepan over high heat.

7. Bring to a boil, beat constantly until the sauce thickens for 2 to 3 minutes. Remove from heat put aside

8. Prepare the rice according to the packing instructions. Add the salt.

9. Mix the tofu with the soy sauce mixture. Decorate with tofu. Sprinkle with scallions and sesame.

Air Fryer Potato Chips

Ingredients

- 1 medium Russet potato, unpeeled, 1/8-inch-thick slice

- 1 tablespoon of rapeseed oil

- 1/4 teaspoon sea salt

- 1/4 teaspoon freshly ground black pepper

- Canola oil

- 1 teaspoon chopped fresh rosemary

COOKING METHOD:

1. In a large bowl of cold water, soak the potato slices for 20 minutes.

2. Drain the potatoes; Dry with paper towels.

3. Clean the container. Then add the oil, salt and pepper.

4. Add the potatoes; Mix well to cover.

5. Lightly coat the air fryer basket with cooking spray.

6. Place half of the potato slices on the basket and cook at 190°C until well cooked and crispy.

7. Work in two batches.

8. Carefully remove the chips with a pair of tongs from the fryer.

9. Sprinkle with rosemary; Serve immediately.

Air Fryer Shrimp Spring Rolls

Ingredients

- 1+1 1/2 tablespoons of sesame oil,

- 2 cups of pre-shredded cabbage

- 1 cup of small carrots

- 1 cup of paprika

- 4 ounces raw shrimp peeled and deveined chopped

- 3/4 cup peas

- 1/4 cup freshly chopped coriander

- 1 tablespoon of lemon juice

- 2 teaspoons fish sauce

- 1/4 teaspoon chopped red pepper

- spring rolls (8 square inches)

- 1/2 cup sweet chili sauce

COOKING METHOD:

1. Heat 1 1/2 teaspoons of oil in a large pan over high heat.

2. Add the cabbage, carrots and pepper; fry with constant stirring until the mixture is slightly withered for 1 to 1 1/2 minutes.

3. Spread on a baking sheet and let it cool for 5 minutes.

4. Put the herb mixture, shrimp, peas, cilantro, lemon juice, fish sauce and chopped red pepper in a large bowl. Mix

5. Place the spring roll with the corner facing you on the work surface.

6. Place 1/4 cup of filler in the middle of each quill assembly and stretch it from left to right onto a long 3-inch strip.

7. Fold the lower corner of each lid over the filling by folding the corner point under the filling.

8. Fold the left and right corners over the filling. Lightly scrub the rest of the corner with water; Roll the full end into the remaining corner. Press lightly to seal.

9. Brush the spring rolls with the remaining 1 tablespoons of oil.

10. Place 4 spring rolls in the frying basket and bake at 180°C until golden brown (6 to 7 minutes) and turn after 5 minutes.

11. Serve with sweet chilli sauce.

Air Fryer Banana Chips

Ingredients

- Four raw bananas

- Black pepper

- salt

- Little oil for the air fryer

COOKING METHOD:

1. Peel the bananas and cut into thin piece

2. place the contents in an air fryer

3. air fry for 10 minutes at 180°C

4. Once finished, sprinkle with salt and pepper.

Air Fryer Chickpeas

Ingredients

- 1 cup Boiled chickpeas

- Salt to taste

- 1 tablespoon cumin powder.

- 1 teaspoon Red pepper powder.

- 1 tbsp Dry Mango powder.

- 1 teaspoon chat Masala

- 1 teaspoon Black salt

- Turmeric a pinch

COOKING METHOD:

1. Take a cup of boiled peas, add all the ingredients and mix well.

2. Air fry at 200°C for 10 minutes, then another 10 minutes at 180°C

3. Serve as a snack.

Air Fryer Monte Cristo

Ingredients

- 1 egg
- ¼ teaspoon vanilla extract
- 2 slices of sourdough bread
- 2½ ounces of Swiss cheese
- 2 ounces of slice ham
- 2 ounces Sliced turkey
- 1 teaspoon of melted butter
- powdered sugar
- Raspberry jam, to serve

COOKING METHOD:

1. Mix the egg and the vanilla extract in a shallow bowl.

2. Put the bread on the counter.

3. Prepare a sandwich with a slice of Swiss cheese, ham, turkey and then a second slice of Swiss cheese on a slice of bread.

4. Cover with the other slice of bread and squeeze lightly to make it flat.

5. Preheat the fryer to 175°C.

6. Cut out a piece of aluminium foil the same size as the bread and brush with melted butter.

7. Dip both sides of the sandwich into the egg mass.

8. Let the dough soak the bread on each side for about 30 seconds.

9. Put the sandwich in the greased aluminium foil and transfer it to the frying basket.

10. For an extra tan, brush the top of the sandwich with melted butter. Roast for 10 minutes at 175°C.

11. Turn the sandwich over, brush with butter and fry in the air for another 8 minutes.

12. Put the sandwich on a plate and sprinkle with powdered sugar. Serve with raspberry or blackberry jam.

Air Fryer Nutella Sandwich

Ingredients

- soft butter

- 4 slices of white bread

- ¼ cup hazelnut chocolate Nutella

- 1 banana

COOKING METHOD:

1. Preheat the fryer to 190°C.

2. Spread the soft butter on one side of all slices of bread and place the butter slices on the counter.

3. Spread the hazelnut chocolate on the other side of the slices of bread.

4. Cut the banana thin layers.

5. Lay the banana slices on two slices of bread and cover with the remaining slices of bread to make two sandwiches.

6. Cut the sandwiches in half.

7. Transfer the sandwiches to the air fryer.

8. Fry for 5 minutes at 190°C.

9. Turn the sandwiches over and fry them for 2-3 minutes in the air, or until the slices of bread are browned.

10. Serve and enjoy!

Air Fryer Sweet Potato Wedges

Ingredients

- 2 big sweet potatoes

- 1 tablespoon Mexican spice

- 1 teaspoon of cumin

- 1 teaspoon mustard powder

- 1 teaspoon chili powder

- 1 tablespoon of olive oil

- Salt

- Pepper

COOKING METHOD:

1. Peel your sweet potatoes and cut them into wedges.

2. preheat your fryer at 180°C for 5 minutes in the air.

3. Add all the spices in a bowl and mix well. Add the potato wedges and mix the spices until well covered.

4. Place the potato quarters in the air fryer, add olive oil and cook for 20 minutes.

5. shake it every 5 minutes until cooked.

6. serve

Air Fryer Pizza Bread Sticks

Ingredients

- 1/3 pizza dough

- 1/2 teaspoon dried coconut powder

- 2 Tablespoons Coconut oil.

- 1 teaspoon Garlic puree

- 25g of cheddar cheese

- Optional bread seeds

- 1 teaspoon of parsley

- Salt and pepper

COOKING METHOD:

1. Start by melting the coconut oil in a small pot.

2. It is best to do this over medium heat until you have a liquid.

3. Add your seasoning and garlic puree and mix well.

4. Lower the pizza dough and give it a thick stick shape.

5. brush coat with oil until well covered.

6. Sprinkle some dried coconut on the top.

7. Add a pinch of cheddar cheese and finish with bread seeds.

8. air dry for 10 minutes at 180°C, then for another 5 minutes at 200°C or until it is cooked in the middle and nice crunchy outside.

Air Fryer Apple Chips

Ingredients

- medium sized apple

- ¼ teaspoon cinnamon

- ¼ teaspoon nutmeg

COOKING METHOD:

1. Preheat the air fryer to 190°C.

2. Finely chop the apple with a knife.

3. Combine apple slices, cinnamon and nutmeg in a bowl.

4. Transfer the spiced apple slices to the frying basket in one layer and bake for 8 minutes. (flip the chips after 4 mins)

Air Fryer Cheese Sticks

Ingredients

- 1-pound mozzarella, block

- 2 eggs

- 3 tablespoons skimmed milk

- 0.25 cup flour, white

- 1 cup of breadcrumbs, nature

COOKING METHOD:

1. Cut the cheese into 3 x 1/2-inch sticks.

2. Put the breadcrumbs in a bowl. Mix the egg and milk and place in another bowl.

3. Dip the cheese sticks into the egg mixture and then into the breadcrumbs.

4. Place the breaded sticks on a baking tray.

5. Freeze in the freezer for 1-2 hours or until frozen.

6. Put small amounts of breaded sticks in the fry basket.

7. Air fry for 12 minutes on 200°C.

8. serve hot!

Air Fryer Roasted Carrots

Ingredients

- Cut 3 cups of carrots into small pieces

- 1 tablespoon of olive oil

- 1 tablespoon of honey

- salt and pepper.

COOKING METHOD:

1. In a bowl, mix the carrots with honey and olive oil.

2. Make sure the carrots are well covered.

3. Season with salt and pepper.

4. Bake in the air fryer for 12 minutes at 200°C.

5. Serve hot.

Air Fryer Chocolate Chip Cookie

Ingredients

- 100 g of butter

- 75 g brown sugar

- 175 g of self-rising flour

- 100 g of chocolate

- 2 tablespoons of honey soup

- 1 tablespoon of milk

COOKING METHOD:

1. Preheat the air fryer to 180°C.

2. Beat butter in a large bowl until soft, add sugar and mix until soft and fluffy.

3. Smash the chocolate with a rolling pin to get a mix of medium and very small chunks of chocolate

4. Add honey and flour and mix well.

5. Add the chocolate.

6. And milk and mix well.

7. Pour the cookie mixture in the air fryer on a baking sheet and bake for six minutes at 180°C.

8. Reduce the temperature for another 2 minutes to 160°C, so that they can cook in the middle.

9. Serve.

Air Fryer Chicken Tender

Ingredients

- 1 pound of raw chicken fillets

- 1/2 cup panko breadcrumbs

- 1 egg

- 1/2 teaspoon garlic puree

- olive oil

- pepper

COOKING METHOD:

1. Season the chicken fillets with the garlic and pepper.

2. Dip the chicken fillets into the egg and cover on both sides.

3. Roll each chicken fillet into panko breadcrumbs. Apply evenly.

4. Put some olive oil on the bottom of the frying pan and add 6-7 steaks to the tray.

5. Set your air fryer to 200°C and cook for 20 minutes.

6. serve

Air Fryer Tofu Salad

Ingredients

- 1 block of tofu cut into pieces

- 2 tablespoons soy sauce

- 1+1 tablespoon of olive oil

- 1 teaspoon turmeric

- 1/2 teaspoon of garlic powder

- 1/2 teaspoon onion powder

- 1/2 cup chopped onion

- 2 1/2 cups of chopped red potatoes

COOKING METHOD:

1. In a medium bowl mix tofu, soy sauce, olive oil, turmeric, garlic powder, onion powder and onion. Set aside for marinating.

2. Mix potatoes with olive oil in a small, small bowl and fry at 200°C for 15 minutes in the air fryer.

3. shake once, about 7 to 8 minutes while cooking.

4. Shake the potatoes again and then add the tofu with the remaining marinade.

5. Fry Tofu and potatoes for another 15 minutes at 180°C.

Air Fryer Chicken Tikka

Ingredients

- 1 pound of chicken thighs (cut into cubes)//
- 1/2 cup Greek yogurt
- 1 teaspoon Garam Masala
- 1 teaspoon curry powder
- 1/2 teaspoon Smoked paprika

- 1/4 teaspoon Cayenne pepper (optional)

- 1 tablespoon of olive oil

- 1 teaspoon salt

- oil spray

- 1 large bell pepper, chopped (optional)

- Big red onion, big cubes (optional),

- lemons and coriander for garnish.

COOKING METHOD:

1. Combine chicken cubes, yoghurt, curry powder, garam masala, smoked paprika, cayenne pepper, olive oil and salt in a large bowl or resealable bag.

2. Give it a good mix and let it marinate in the fridge for 2 hours.

3. Skewer each cube with red onion chunks and green pepper chunks and add a piece of chicken alternately with green pepper and red onion

4. Lightly grease the frying basket.

5. Put the skewers in the basket and fry in 182°C for 15 minutes.

6. Serve chicken tikka with a dash of lemon juice and a pinch of chopped cilantro.

Air Fryer Sweet Pot Tot

Ingredients

- 2 small 14 oz. Sweet potatoes, peeled

- 1 tablespoon of potato starch

- 1/8 teaspoon garlic powder

- 1 1/4 teaspoon kosher salt, divided

- 3/4 cup tomato sauce without added salt

- cooking spray

COOKING METHOD:

1. Boil water in a medium pot over high heat.

2. Add potatoes and cook until they are tender, for about 15 minutes.

3. Transfer the potatoes to a plate and let them cool, for about 15 minutes.

4. Grate the potatoes in a medium bowl with the big holes of an all-in-one grater.

5. Carefully mix with potato starch, garlic powder and 1 teaspoon of salt.

6. Make the mixture into 24 nuggets. Coat the basket with cooking spray.

7. work in batches, put half (about 12) in a single layer inside the basket and spray with cooking spray.

8. Bake at 200°C until lightly browned (12 to 14 minutes).

9. Remove from the frying basket and sprinkle with 1/8 teaspoon of salt.

10. Repeat with the rest of them. Serve immediately with tomato sauce.

Air Fryer Banana Bread

Ingredients

- 3/4 cup (3 ounces) Whole Wheat Flour

- 1 teaspoon of cinnamon

- 1/2 teaspoon kosher salt

- 1/4 teaspoon baking soda

- 2 ripe medium bananas (total 12 ounces), minced

- 2 big eggs lightly beaten

- 1/2 cup granulated sugar

- 1/3 cup low-fat natural yogurt

- 2 tablespoons vegetable oil

- 1 teaspoon of vanilla extract

- 2 tablespoons (3/4 oz) toasted walnuts,

- cooking spray

COOKING METHOD:

1. Lay the bottom of a round 6-inch cake pan with parchment paper;

2. Cover the pan lightly with cooking spray.

3. Mix the flour, cinnamon, salt and baking powder in a medium bowl; put aside

4. Mix the mashed banana, eggs, sugar, yogurt, oil and vanilla in a separate bowl.

5. Carefully pour the mixture into the flour and mix until it is smooth.

6. Put the dough in the prepared pan and sprinkle with nuts.

7. Preheat the fryer at 155°C, then place the pan in the fryer and bake until it is golden brown for about 30 mins.

8. Insert a wooden stick in the centre, if it comes out clean its ready to serve, if not then let it bake for 5-10 mins more.

Air Fryer Hash Brown

Ingredients

- Potatoes, large - 4 - peeled and finely grated

- Cornmeal - 2 tablespoons

- Salt – taste

- Pepper powder – taste

- Chilli flakes - 2 teaspoon tea

- Garlic powder - 1 teaspoon (optional

- Onion powder - 1 teaspoon (optional)

- Vegetable oil - 1 + 1 teaspoon

COOKING METHOD:

1. Soak the grated potatoes in cold water.

2. Drain the water. Repeat this step to drain the excess starch from the potatoes.

3. In a coated pan, heat 1 teaspoon of vegetable oil and fry the grated potatoes until lightly cooked for 3-4 minutes.

4. Allow the potatoes to cool and place on a plate.

5. Add the cornmeal, salt, pepper, garlic and onion powder, chilli flakes and mix well.

6. Spread it on the plate and beat it firmly with your fingers.

7. Let cool for 20 minutes.

8. Preheat the fryer to 180°C.

9. Take the potato and divide it evenly with a knife

10. Brush the basket of the fryer with little oil.

11. Place the pieces of hash brown in the basket and bake for 15 minutes at 180°C

12. Remove the basket and return the fried potatoes after 6 minutes to fry them evenly.

13. Serve hot with ketchup.

About Author

Shahbaaz is an entrepreneur, motivational speaker, bodybuilder and an author.

He has competed in various bodybuilding competitions. He is a fitness expert.

Shahbaaz's primary focus, through his book is to help everyone around the world to become fit, healthy and live a happy life.

Shahbaaz is the bestselling author of *"EASY AIR FRYER COOKBOOK RECIPES"*.

ONE LAST THING

If you really enjoyed this book or find it useful. I'd be really grateful if you write short review on Amazon. Your support really does make a difference and I read all your reviews personally. So I can get your feedback and make this book even better.

If you would like to leave a review all you have to do is go to amazon and open my book and scroll down to write a review.